WAVES OF INSPIRATIONAL QUOTES ON

THE SUPER NATURAL

WAVES OF INSPIRATIONAL QUOTES

ON

SUPERNATURAL

By

Sekudo Michael Ajiboye

PUBLICATION

This piece is the original work of the author. No part of this book is permitted to be reproduced or used for publication, intellectual discuss without permission and reference to the author of this book.

APPRECIATION

All gratitude goes to God who is the Giver of wisdom and understanding, for the inspiration given to put this together and for this piece to be a blessing to others. My appreciation goes to my lovely wife and my children for sacrificing their time and comfort at the moment of working on this book.

I wish to sincerely appreciate the impacts of my spiritual fathers: Bishop David Oyedepo and Bishop David Abioye, my mentors, seniors, leaders, friends, well wishers and colleagues in the work of the ministry for the inspiration, words of encouragement and support received towards this publication.

I will not forget to acknowledge the effort of my graphic designer Daniel Agboje, who typed, compiled and designed the content of this book. My sincere appreciation goes to the CEO of MIKETOJANE PRINTING AND PUBLISHING LIMITED for editing, professional packaging and publishing of the book.

INTRODUCTION

Inspirations are products of divine revelations delivered by the Spirit of God to man; documented to impact and transform others. This publication is a product of such Revelational experience. Be blessed as you go through this piece of work.

SEKUDO MICHAEL AJIBOYE

@michaelajiboye4@gmail.com
@msekudo(Twitter)
michaelajiboyesekudo(Instagram)
www.d-blossomsupernaturalhighways.org.ng

" IN FULFILLING YOUR DESTINY, YOU'RE
MOVED BY WHAT YOU SEE AND NOT WHAT
YOU FEEL.

"GOD DOES NOT ANNOUNCE MEN BECAUSE
THEY ARE GOOD, RATHER HE ANNOUNCES THEM
BECAUSE THEY ARE DUE."

" WHEN THE PRESENCE OF GOD
IS AT WORK IN ANY BATTLE,
CONQUEST BY THE ENEMY
IS NOT IN VIEW."

" ANYTIME GOD WANTS TO SHOWCASE YOU FOR
A MIRACLE, HE PERMITS A PROBLEM
SOMEWHERE AND PUT THE SOLUTION INSIDE
YOU... UNTIL YOU'RE LOCATED, NO SOLUTION."

" YOU CAN DO MANY THINGS AND HAVE
NOTHING; AND YOU CAN DO ONE THING AND
HAVE MANY THINGS... LOVE IS THAT ONE THING
THAT QUALIFIES YOU FOR MANY THINGS."

" THE STRENGTH OF MAN MAY DETERMINE THE PROCESS OF LABOUR, IT IS THE GRACE OF GOD THAT DETERMINES THE PRODUCT OF LABOUR."

" DIVINE SETTLEMENT IS A COVENANT WORD
THAT DEFINES THE MOVEMENT OF A MAN
FROM A POINT OF TURBULENCE TO
CONVENIENCE."

" DIVINE SETTLEMENT CONNOTES RECEIVING
YOUR RIGHT ACCORDING TO YOUR DESIRED-SIZE
IN YOUR APPOINTED SEASON ."

" WHEN GOD WANTS TO CHANGE YOUR STORY
HE REPOSITIONS YOUR LIFE
TO THE DIRECTION OF A NEW GLORY."

" THE SUPERNATURAL IS A SPIRITUAL REALM
WHERE THE COMMON MAN
HEARS UNCOMMON VOICE,
THE COMMON EYES
SEES UNCOMMON THINGS,
AND THE NATURAL MIND
ENCOUNTERS UNCOMMON
EXPERIENCES."

" TO HAVE A SOLID SPIRITUAL BASE WITH GOD,
THREE FACTORS MUST BE OPERATING IN YOUR
LIFE CONCURRENTLY: RELATIONSHIP WITH GOD,
WITH THE WORD AND ADHERENCE TO A
TEACHING PRIEST."

" LET GOD FIGHT, ANYTIME HE FIGHTS, THE
CAMP OF THE ENEMY WILL BE TIGHT... ANYTIME
HE FIGHTS THE ENEMY MUST LOSE HIS SIGHT...
ANYTIME HE FIGHTS THE ENEMY MUST REDUCE
IN SIZE."

" IN SPIRITUAL WARFARE,
CRYING TO GOD EXPRESSES
YOUR FEELINGS... PRAYING IN FAITH
EXPRESSES YOUR CONFIDENCE IN HIM."

" TESTIMONIES ARE GOD'S CONSTANT ABILITY IN
MAN'S INABILITY, TO PROVE HIS POSSIBILITY IN
THE MIDST OF MAN'S IMPOSIBILITES ."

" THE GIFT OF DISCERNMENT IS THE
MANIFESTATION OF THE SUPERNATURAL, THAT
HELPS TO DISTINGUISH BETWEEN WHAT IS GOOD
AND WHAT IS RIGHT."

" THE SUPERNATURAL ANNOUCES THE ARRIVAL
OF GOD IN ANY SITUATION ; BUT HIS DEPARTURE
IS MADE MANIFEST WHEN MAN LIVES
CONSTANTLY WITHOUT THE PRESENCE,
VISITATION, ACTS AND TESTIMONIES OF GOD IN
HIS LIFE.."

" THE SUPERNATURAL INITIATES THE SPIRIT OF
GOD INTO THE HEART OF MAN, TO CHANGE HIS
THINKING TOWARDS GOD AND HIS SITUATION
FOR BETTER RESULT IN LIFE."

" THE SUPERNATURAL IS A HEAVENLY FORCE
THAT PROVES THE SUPREMACY OF GOD OVER
MAN AND HIS SITUATION, THE RESPONSE OR
REACTION OF MAN NOT WITHSTANDING."

" THE SUPERNATURAL REALM
IS AN EXPERIENCE THAT AWAKENS
THE SPIRIT OF MAN TO BE
CONSCIOUS OF GOD."

"THE POWER OF WILLINGNESS
IS THE GATEWAY TO
GOD'S USEFULNESS."

" THE SUPERNATURAL IS THE NATURAL
HABITAT OF GOD FOR COMMANDING
STRANGE ACTS AMONG MEN."

“ YOU MUST SEE WHAT GOD IS SEEING
BEFORE YOU CAN HAVE WHAT GOD IS”.
SAYING. ”

" YOUR SPIRITUAL WEIGHT DETERMINES
YOUR SPIRITUAL MARK."

" PRAYER IS AN EXCHANGE OF POSITION
BETWEEN MAN AND GOD
TO LIVE A NEW LIFE. "

" ANYTIME YOU ENCOUNTER
GOD'S GLORY, IT CHANGES YOUR STORY
AND GIVES YOU A NEW NATURE."

" UNTIL YOUR LIFE BECOMES STRAIGHT,
YOUR CASE MAY NOT BE LAY TO REST,
SELF-DECEIT IS SELF-AFFLICTION."

" KNOWLEDGE IS A SOURCE OF STRENGTH FOR
RELEVANCE."

"IF GOD IS NOT INVOLVED
IN YOUR HEALING PLAN, THEN HIS HANDS MAY
NOT BE INVOLVED IN YOUR RESCUE."

" WHERE YOU'RE RAISED,
DETERMINES WHERE YOU'RE PLACED."

"WHEN GRACE IS AT WORK, HUMAN ERROR
CAN'T BE A BARRIER TO DIVINE COLOUR AND
HONOUR."

" WHEN YOU LOSE TOUCH WITH DIVINE SIGNAL,
YOU WILL NEVER HAVE A TOUCH WITH DIVINE
SIGNS .

" WHEN THE GRACE OF GOD
IS SUFFICIENT, THE RACE OF LIFE
WILL BE CONVENIENT."

" I AM BORN TO BE BLESSED, REDEEMED TO BE SUCCESSFUL AND BY COVENANT TO BE PROSPEROUS."

" WHEN ONE THING THAT IS NEEDFUL
IS DONE, ALL OTHER
THINGS WILL BE USEFUL."

" EVERY TURNING POINT WITH GOD
IS A DISCOVERY OF NEW BEGINNING."

" ANYTIME YOU TURN AROUND WITH GOD ,
YOU TURN TO HAVE WHAT IS YOURS."

" DIVINE SETTLEMENT IS AN ACT
OF REFUSING TO BE DEFEATED
SO AS TO BE DECORATED."

" DIVINE SETTLEMENT, IS A DEPARTURE FROM A
TEMPORAL PLACE OF DISCOMFORT TO A
COVENANT DESTINATION OF ABSOLUTE REST."

" THE SUPERNATURAL IS THE REALM OF THE
KINGDOM OF THE HEAVENLY SPIRITS."

" THE SUPERNATURAL IS THE MEETING POINT
BETWEEN THE SPIRIT OF MAN
AND THE SPIRIT OF GOD."

" THE SUPERNATURAL IS A REALM WHERE
THE VOICE OF MAN IS SUSPENDED
TO HEAR AND LISTEN
TO THE VOICE OF GOD."

" IT IS A REALM WHERE TIME & SEASON
MEET WITH ETERNITY;
IN THAT PLACE YOU DON'T GET TIRED."

"THERE IS NO FAVOURITE WITH GOD, THE DAY YOU MEET HIS DEMANDS, HE DELIVERS YOUR REQUEST."

" THERE IS NO REGRET(S), WHEN GOD'S DEFENSE IS YOUR SURE FOUNDATION."

" THE SUPERNATURAL IS A REALM WHERE
CARNALITY DIES EFFORTLESSLY."

" THE SUPERNATURAL IS A REALM WHERE
YOU CARRY THE GLORY
TO TERMINATE YOUR GROANING."

" WHEN RELEVANCE TAKES THE LEAD
IN THE LIFE OF ANY MAN, PRODUCTIVITY AND
CURRENCY OF IMPACT IS INEVITABLE. ."

" WHEN GOD'S PRESENCE GOES WITH YOU, THE
DISAPPOINTMENT OF YOUR ENEMIES WILL BE
WRITTEN IN
CAPITAL LETTERS ."

" YOUR INTERNAL AND EXTERNAL FULFILLMENT
IN LIFE BEGINS WITH YOUR SPIRITUAL
RELATIONSHIP WITH GOD."

" UNTIL YOUR SPIRIT MAN
FINDS REST IN GOD, YOUR ENTIRE LIFE
CAN'T FIND REST WITH GOD."

" THE MORE YOU ENJOY THE GRACE OF A PRIEST,
THE LESS YOUR SPIRITUAL RISK."

" THE WORD OF GOD IS THE EXPRESSION
OF THE HEART OF GOD.
ANYTHING HE SAYS, HE WILL DO."

" THE VOICE OF GOD IS STRONGER
THAN THE PEN OF MEN."

" THE VOICE OF GOD IS MIGHTIER
THAN THE SOUND OF WAR."

" THE WORD OF GOD IS THE LIFE OF GOD
EXPRESSED THROUGH CHRIST TO REDEEM MAN
FROM THE CRISIS OF LIFE."

" THE WORD IS THE SPIRIT
OF GOD TRANSFERRED INTO
MAN THROUGH THE SPOKEN WORD."

" WHEN GOD ROARS,
HEAVEN STRIKES."

" WHEN GOD SOUND FROM HEAVEN,
SATAN SINK ON THE EARTH. "

" THE SUPERNATURAL IS
THE SEAT OF GOD, WHERE
THE HEAT OF MAN IS TERMINATED."

" WHEN THE WONDERS OF
GOD VISIT A WANDERER,
HE/SHE BECOMES A CELEBRITY."

" THE SUPERNATURAL IS THE
'FACE OF GOD' IN THE 'CASE OF MAN."

" THE SUPERNATURAL ANNOUCES THE MOVE OF
GOD TO MAKE YOU
A BETTER PERSON."

" THE SUPERNATURAL ANNOUNCES
THE ABILITY OF GOD TO
GIVE YOU A POSSESSION."

" THE SUPERNATURAL ANNOUNCES THE ACTS OF
GOD TO GIVE YOU A SOLUTION."

" THE SUPERNATURAL ANNOUCES
THE WAYS OF GOD TO GIVE
YOU A DIRECTION."

" THE SUPERNATURAL IS
GOD AT WORK, THROUGH HIS
WORD TO GIVE YOU A WORTH."

" ALL ROUND REST IS THE COVENANT OF
PEACE AT WORK IN THE MIDST OF STORMS ."

" THE SUPERNATURAL ANNOUCES
THE VOICE OF GOD TO
GAIN YOUR ATTENTION."

" WHEN GRACE IS AT WORK,
A MAN OF AFFLICTION
CAN BECOME A MAN OF ATTRACTION & AFFECTION".

" WHEN GRACE IS AT WORK,
A MAN OF DEMOTION
CAN BECOME A MAN OF EXPANSION."

ABOUT THE BOOK

The supernatural is a realm where the common man hears uncommon voice, sees uncommon things, the mind encounters uncommon experiences. That's what becomes your new spiritual ideology as you go through the collections of words on the 'SUPERNATURAL' documented in this book.

ABOUT THE AUTHOR

The author, SEKUDO MICHAEL AJIBOYE, is a seasoned minister of the gospel for more than a decade with Living Faith Church, Worldwide, a.k.a. Winners' Chapel. Under the leadership of his spiritual parents, Bishop (Dr.) David Oyedepo, Pst. (Mrs) Faith Oyedepo and Bishop David Abioye. The spiritual mentorship and impartation received from them contributed to a very large extent to the inspiration that birth this book.

He has an unsual dimension of teaching grace. His teaching virtue is not just a CALLING but also a MINISTRY. His continuos versatility in pastoral work, coupled with intellectual prowess and experience, is what informs his unique pattern of ministration. Listening to him is without regrets. He's often celebrated by his audience and admirers. Reading from him will be quite impactful.